T0123379

LIVING AND

DYING WITH ALZHEIMER'S

And Related Diseases

Frances Hightower

A Compelling Story by a Family Caregiver

Order this book online at www.trafford.com
or email orders@trafford.com

Most Trafford titles are also available at major online book retailers.

Note for Librarians: A cataloguing record for this book is available from Library
and Archives Canada at www.collectionscanada.ca/amicus/index-e.html

Printed in Victoria, BC, Canada.

ISBN: 9781-4251-7724-9

*Our mission is to efficiently provide the world's finest, most comprehensive
book publishing service, enabling every author to experience success.
To find out how to publish your book, your way, and have it available
worldwide, visit us online at www.trafford.com*

Trafford rev. 8/28/2009

 www.trafford.com

North America & international
toll-free: 1 888 232 4444 (USA & Canada)
phone: 250 383 6864 ♦ fax: 812 355 4082

TABLE OF CONTENTS

INTRODUCTION

"Well, Mama couldn't take it anymore so she upped an' died."

That was Skippy's explanation when our Mama died of Alzheimer's in 1994. Skippy was retarded and lived all of his sixty-four years with his mother and father in the family home. Two younger siblings lived only a few blocks away.

"What are we gonna do now?" Skippy had a way of sounding very pitiful when he asked this. Daddy answered, "We'll tough it out."

This story tells how our family used strong doses of humor to "tough it out" through Skippy's disabilities, Mama's Alzheimer's, and, most recently, Daddy's cancer.

CHAPTER 1

SOMETHING WAS WRONG

The phone on my office desk rang. It was Mama. I could hardly hear her.

"Frances," she whispered. Her voice was quivering and raspy. She was over seventy years old and had many ills, but until now nothing had affected her voice. I pushed the phone harder to my ear and strained to hear as she continued.

"Someone has broken into the house." She paused, sighed, and her voice got weaker. "They're downstairs. I can hear them talking. Come home now. Hurry, I'm scared."

Click. The dial tone was almost deafening. It jolted me back to reality. Call her back? No. Call the police? Call the neighbors? I did both as quickly as my mind would function. Then I grabbed my purse, explained that I had an emergency, and rushed out the door.

My heart was beating faster than I could drive on the two-lane road winding through the Virginia countryside. I usually enjoyed the twenty-mile drive to and from work, but now it seemed more like two hundred miles as I heard Mama's voice saying, "Hurry, I'm scared."

Just last week I had brought Mama from Florida to stay with me while Daddy was rebuilding their house, which had been destroyed by fire. Losing the home they had built in the 1930s and everything they owned was the most recent disaster to strike my family.

We had learned long ago to cope with crises, to endure, survive, and go on. Daddy was a rock. He always picked up the pieces and, with worn out tools, began again. Mama was a fighter. Like a grizzly bear, she fiercely protected her cubs. She was determined that we would have a normal life–against unbelievable odds. Skippy, my older brother, was "not normal". That was the least cruel term used in 1930 to describe someone born with a disability. I was born four years later, and Brother William came in with the March winds of 1947.

I took a deep breath and tried to control my thoughts as I waited at the only traffic light in the town of Orange. Finally, I approached the two-story white clapboard house that I had purchased ten years before when I was living and working in Washington, D.C.. There was a police car at the curb, neighbors on the porch, and children poking curiously around the yard.

Everyone started talking to me at once as I got out of the car. The front door was locked; no sign of a break-in. There did not appear to be anyone in the house except Mama, and she would not answer. I unlocked the door and rushed upstairs to the guest bedroom in the back of the house. Mama was in bed, reading. She glanced up and smiled at me. "Well, hello," she said cheerfully, "what are you doing home this time of day?" I stared at her. Her hair had been jet black and below her waist when it wasn't braided or in a fashionable pompadour. Frequent hospitalizations had necessitated a short, more easily managed hairstyle, and the years had shaded the black to tones of grey. She hated the grey. She hated everything about being old and did not accept it gracefully. A smooth magnolia complexion belied her age. Below a knitted brow, the eyelids drooped slightly over mahogany eyes that were intense, even through the clear-rimmed glasses.

Everything was just as I had left it that morning–a Coke on the bedside table and, next to the telephone, a large note with my office telephone number.

Mama sensed my anxiety now and sat up in bed. "Is something wrong?" she asked with sincere innocence.

"You called me about someone being in the house," I said slowly and watched for her reaction.

"I didn't call you. Who's been in the house?"

I felt like I was in the twilight zone. I tried again.

"Mama, you called me at my office and said someone had broken into the house and I should come home right away. Do you remember that?"

"I haven't called anyone. I've been right here in bed all morning reading my book. I'm just fine. You didn't have to come home because of me. Have you had your lunch?"

Mama wasn't scared anymore. But I was. That was just the beginning.

CHAPTER 2

THE EARLY GOODBYE

Over the next week, I realized that Mama was weaving in and out of reality. I chalked it up to old age and memory loss, but the events became more and more bizarre and difficult to handle. Mercifully, most of the lurid details have escaped my memory, but they took a toll on my emotions.

I was all right until after I put Mama on the plane to fly back home to Florida. The agent had let me help Mama board the plane and get settled into her seat. As I left her, Mama and I both smiled and fought back tears. I stood at the huge glass window inside the terminal and waved as the plane pulled away from the gate. I was mesmerized as the plane taxied to the runway, made its turn, and slowly lifted into the air. It climbed into the clouds and became only a speck in the sky.

When I could see the plane no more, I began to cry uncontrollably. I was on the verge of hysteria and could not stop crying. My brain would not function. Where was my car? How could I drive home like this? Orange was ninety miles away.

People stared at me as I began to walk aimlessly toward nowhere. I stumbled into a telephone booth and sat there trying to remember the phone number of anyone I could call for help. Everything was blurred, but a familiar number came to mind. I dialed. A friendly voice answered. He listened to my incoherent babbling and sobbing. Ron had known me long enough to realize this was most abnormal behavior. He did not ask for explanations. "Where are you?" he asked calmly. I told him. "Wait right there. I'm on my way." His voice was reassuring, but not enough to stop the tears and sobs. I waited, oblivious to time or people or the incessant hubbub of airport noises. When Ron found me, I was still crying. I don't know when I stopped or why. Perhaps my eyes had dehydrated, if that's possible.

Mama died in January of 1994, after thirteen years in the abysmal hell we now know as Alzheimer's. I cried, of course, but my loss of Mama began the day I said goodbye to her at the airport.

CHAPTER 3

THE CONTRAST

That was spring of 1981. Mama had just turned seventy-three. For more than twenty-five years, she had tenaciously fought mysterious illnesses, emotional distress, and five major surgeries, the last of which resulted in a colostomy.

Before retiring from state government at the age of seventy, she was, in her own words, "the best damn legal secretary in the State of Florida," and everyone agreed. She took dictation at one hundred twenty words per minute, typed (not on a computer) almost that fast, and rarely made a mistake. She worked crossword puzzles in ink.

Her emotions had always been like a roller coaster. She could live life to the fullest and savor every minute when she was happy. Those times became fewer and farther apart as the years went by. More often, she wrestled with pain, depression, and anger.

Her one indulgence in life was food. She hated being overweight–or fat, as she bluntly put it–but she knew her limitations and made no pretense of dieting. A very proud and striking person, she had always been immaculate in appearance, always coordinating apparel, costume jewelry, shoes, and accessories. A slight scent of Yardley's English Roses announced her presence.

I remember all of this in stark contrast to the person she became as Alzheimer's took its toll. As the disease progressed, we would cling to any glimpses of Mama being "normal", although the definition of normal changed from month to month.

Sometimes a situation can be so indescribably horrible that the only possible reaction is laughter. Unless you have experienced this, it sounds cruel, but it is survival. It is the mind's way of dealing with something that is otherwise totally unacceptable. They say that laughter is therapeutic, that laughter is an escape. We learned to laugh a lot.

CHAPTER 4

THE DISEASE

Most people have little concept of Alzheimer's disease. They think it is just memory loss, like an absent-minded professor who can't find his glasses or calendar. How bad can that be?

Perhaps this misconception occurs because people who experience the impact of Alzheimer's cannot bring themselves to share their experiences with others. But some choose to describe the nightmare by writing about it. Some books and articles on the subject are very graphic. It was hard for me to read them.

One article began: "How would you react if you saw your mother blow her nose on a slice of bread?" Your first reaction may be horror. Gradually, as this habit repeats, you accept it. Then there's the frightening realization that this behavior seems almost normal in comparison to what eventually happens as the disease progresses.

Mama didn't blow her nose on bread. She twisted a whole tissue of Kleenex into two small spirals with the ends flared and stuffed one end up each nostril. I began to doubt my sanity when I was no longer bothered by this most unusual sight.

There is a common thread that seems to affect all Alzheimer's patients. "I want to go home" is a phrase caregivers hear repeatedly, but it's impossible to determine where home is. For five years, Mama wanted to go home. All that time, she was in the only home she had known for over fifty years; still she wanted to go home. She could not describe home. It wasn't necessarily where she lived as a child, or an earlier house that she and Daddy had shared. Sometimes she said it was where the children were, obviously a place from the past that existed only in her mind.

When Mama was still able to walk, she prepared to "go home" each night by packing all of her clothes and putting her suitcases on the front porch. One night, I found her sitting in the swing on the porch at 3 a.m. She was waiting for her Pappa to come take her home.

Each morning, we unpacked everything and put it back in the closet. We tried hiding the suitcases; she packed in plastic bags. We were quite surprised one morning to realize that she packed all of Daddy's clothes, too. Packing and unpacking was a household ritual for weeks at a time until another fantasy would take over.

CHAPTER 5

THE LETTER

Skippy was "different". He was short, rotund, had an impish grin, and made faces and funny noises. In public, he attracted attention. People looked at him. People laughed at him. Mama couldn't tolerate this. She got mad and vocal, and she could be very vocal. She and Daddy knew every cuss word any sailor ever used, and then some. Skippy learned every one by heart.

To this day, I don't know the exact medical explanation for Skippy's disability. I've been told that it was a defect that can now be cured at birth. A glandular and/or thyroid deficiency is as close as anyone has come to a definition.

Mama and Daddy did not consider themselves poor because their values were not based on money. When they eloped in 1927, Mama was making a meager salary as a young stenographer in a local law office. Daddy was an electrician for the City and worked as a mechanic after hours. Skippy was born in a small three-room house Daddy built on a lot owned by Mama's family. They had no health insurance, no savings, but, like so many people of that generation, they "got by".

When Skippy was not developing as other children his age, they took him to specialists in Jacksonville and Atlanta. For Skippy and me, these were not dreaded visits to a doctor. Mama and Daddy had a unique way of making ordinary occasions into something special. We planned the trips and anticipated them as great adventures.

I don't know exactly when these trips started or stopped, but they lasted many years after I was born in 1934. I have fond memories of frequent treks to Atlanta–much more than a five-hour drive then. We savored Georgia peaches fresh off the trees and wiped the sweet, sticky juice across our faces. We laughed at the Burma Shave signs each trip as though seeing them for the first time, and eagerly watched for familiar billboards. Our favorite was Fisk Tire Company's little boy in his Dr. Denton pajamas, yawning, holding a lighted candle in one hand and a Fisk tire in the other, with the caption, "It's Time to Retire."

Skippy knew the names of all of his doctors, their nurses, and even the kind little old lady who operated the elevator in the hotel where we stayed. When no one else was on the elevator, she let Skippy turn the lever that controlled UP or DOWN. We laughed and screamed as the elevator came to a jerky stop.

One month, when Skippy was eight or ten, I had the measles, and Mama had to stay home with me while Daddy took Skippy to Atlanta. On that visit, the doctor told Daddy there was nothing more he could do. He said Skippy should be institutionalized. Daddy could not bear the thought of telling Mama, so he asked the doctor to write a letter.

I found that letter many, many years later. I'm not sure whether the yellowing was from age or tears, or both.

The only facility for "people like Skippy" in the 1940s was the State mental institution. This conjured up visions of a horror movie that graphically depicted life in an insane asylum during the early 1900s.

Skippy lived at home, with his family, for sixty-four years.

CHAPTER 6

COPING

Everyone in our family reacted to stress in a different way. Mama vented, said exactly what was on her mind in no uncertain terms. Then she ate to extremes, not one hamburger, but two or three, downed with two giant Cokes and followed with half a box of chocolates. This, of course, produced severe stomach problems, but it never stopped her from repeating the same cycle when she was upset.

Daddy steamed in silence. Without saying a word, he could invoke the darkest clouds that lingered for days. His unspoken anger more than matched Mama's tantrums. I observed that neither the tantrums nor the silence actually relieved the stress or changed whatever started it all. Time would pass and things would be "about normal" again for a while. That was Daddy's description of our family when we were not in the midst of a crisis. As time passed, we gladly accepted the condition of "about normal".

Most of Skippy's stress factors were predictable, but there was very little we could do about them. If it rained on his parade, everyone knew about it–God and all the neighbors. It was even worse if the electricity went out, and woe be unto us if the television went on the blink. Skippy loved to fish, but if the fish didn't bite, or if someone in another boat caught a fish, it was hell to pay. Whatever its origin or meaning, "hell to pay" was a dreaded consequence that we always wanted to avoid.

Skippy's protests were not limited to vocal outbursts. He bit his wrists, pounded on his head with both fists, and pulled at his hair. He became almost completely bald, with only a slight fringe from ear to ear around the back. I've read that these acts are symptomatic of some people with similar disabilities.

Over the years, I have tried almost every conceivable approach to handling stress. One of the most memorable was my first encounter with yoga. This was back when some people (not me, of course!) were still trying to understand the difference between "yoga" and "yogurt".

I signed up for a yoga course at the local community college. Reading over the literature, I learned that I was to wear loose fitting clothes, bring a blanket, and remove my shoes before starting the class.

I missed the first class and was late for the next one because of an unusually stressful day. I signed in and reluctantly took off my shoes. I could detect the smell of sweaty feet. The classroom door noisily announced my arrival, but no one turned to glare at the latecomer. They were transfixed on the instructor at the front of the room as she so clearly enunciated in resonate tones, "Relax. Breathe in through your nose and out through your toes."

I am a logical person. Too logical. Maybe logical people are not supposed to do yoga. Either everyone else in the room was managing to breathe out through their toes, or they were doing a good job of pretending. I don't pretend very well either. While I was still lost in this dilemma, the resonate voice said to get ready for our oohmes.

Fortunately, no one moves very quickly in a yoga class, so I was not conspicuous as I stood perfectly still waiting to see what others were doing. Blankets. Everyone was spreading his blanket. I could do that. Then we sat on crossed legs, palms turned up, eyes closed, as that soft, chimey music drifted into the silence. The room was dark as everyone began to take deep breaths and the oohmes began.

What in the world were they saying? I didn't have a clue. Obviously I missed this in the first class. I decided it was best that I not try to join in, but I saw shadows of figures rocking back and forth. I could do that, too. So I rocked, and listened. A word came to me, "Omar..." Omar something. Then I picked up a few more words, "Omar...shars...ooms." Again, "Omar...shars...ooms... mo..."

Then it came to me and I had to hold my hand over my mouth to stifle laughter. I still don't know what they were saying, but in my mind, it was and always will be: "Omar Shariff's Oldsmobile"–over and over and over again.

I have tried yoga many times since then, and I still can't breathe through my toes. But Omar Shariff's Oldsmobile works every time.

CHAPTER 7

PISS & MOAN

One of our favorite family pastimes was sitting on the front screened porch. We had two old-fashioned porch swings and a rocking chair. Everyone had his own place. The rocker was Skippy's. He sat there for hours and rocked and talked, and rocked and talked, and talked and talked and talked–to no one in particular, about every subject imaginable, in a very loud voice. Actually, he broadcast. His voice was penetrating and he could be heard around the block. Mama always wanted Skippy to be quiet–and he never was.

"Skippy, hush." "Skippy, be quiet." Finally: "Skippy, for God's sake shut up!" I'm not so sure it was for God's sake, or our sake, or the neighbors' sake, but it didn't matter because Skippy would not be quiet. He paused long enough to hear what Mama said and then, like putting a phonograph needle back on the record, he picked up right where he left off, even louder.

When Skippy was mad or upset about something, he would sit on the porch and cuss out God and all of the neighbors, by name, in his broadcast voice. God and the neighbors didn't seem to mind, but it really got to Mama. In the midst of one of these cussing sessions, Mama yelled from her bedroom window: "Skippy! For God's sake stop that pissing and moaning!" There was a very brief moment of silence. Then Skippy resumed his rocking and announced to one and all, "I'm gonna piss and moan, piss and moan, piss and moan!"

To this day, Brother William and I have solved many a problem by sitting on the porch, pissing and moaning.

CHAPTER 8

BASKETS HELL!

Our family was also very steeped in tradition, and it was important for Mama to sit on the porch with us, even though as Alzheimer's progressed, she was not really there most of the time. But on this day she made her presence known in a way that we will never forget.

Mama and Daddy were in one swing. Brother William and I were in the other, and Skippy was in his rocker. We were pretending to "be normal". Brother William and Daddy talked about last night's baseball game; Mama asked why the dog was driving our car; I was trying to make Skippy be quiet. Brother William or Daddy had just said something rather innocuous that got Mama's attention. She suddenly sat upright from her usual slumped position, leaned forward with both fists on her hips, and said with great indignation, in her most normal voice, "BASKETS, HELL!!"

It had nothing to do with anything that had been said or done, but she had her say. Brother William and I laughed so hard we almost fell out of the swing. Skippy stopped talking and looked at Mama in disbelief. He had not heard that tone of voice in a long time. A grin spread across Daddy's face as he lowered his head and tried not to laugh out loud. Mama slowly sank back down in the swing, as if the air was escaping from her balloon. Skippy resumed rocking and broadcasting.

A week or so later, Brother William and I were at the doctor's office with Daddy. We had been there for almost two hours and had a bad case of the waiting room blues. We were tired, frustrated, and impatient. One of the nurses walked by and mumbled something that neither of us understood. Brother William and I looked at each other and said simultaneously, "BASKETS, HELL!"

CHAPTER 9

FIRE & BRIMSTONE

Beginning in the early 1980s, I made many emergency flights to Tallahassee from my home in Virginia, often not knowing what to expect upon arrival. This time I knew–the family home had been destroyed by fire.

Brother William met me at the airport. He gave me the highlights as we drove toward home. Mama, Daddy, and Skippy had gone fishing. As they were driving back and were within a block of the house, they found the street barricaded. A policeman approached the car and began to explain that a house was on fire. He recognized Daddy. "C.J.! It's your house!" Daddy bolted from the car. He looked like an Olympic runner as he headed for the house. Firemen held him back from the charred rubble.

That night, Brother William's small house expanded to accommodate our family of five. There were three bedrooms, but only one double bed and a couch. Skippy was disoriented and complaining bitterly about everything of his that had been destroyed. We were exhausted and stunned. How do you explain devastation like that? It's like being naked in public. You have nothing, have nowhere to go, and don't know where to begin.

We comforted each other with the realization that no one had been hurt. If they had been home, perhaps taking a nap, they could have been killed in the fire. This feeling of relief gradually overcame the grief, and we began to think about what we needed to do next.

The house would be rebuilt, exactly as it was, exactly where it was. That was final, and it was the beginning of many such final decisions Daddy made over the next few months. We learned to recognize the finality of the decisions by the set of his jaw. If we argued, the jaw got firmer, the teeth tighter, the lips thinner. When the jaw began to tremble and the lips turned blue-ish, we backed off.

With a special permit from the City, a mobile home was put in the front yard, just beyond the burned debris. Skippy had recently been diagnosed with diabetes, which had already caused glaucoma, partial blindness and a very unsteady gait. Daddy built a ramp to give Skippy easier access to the trailer. Then he built a crossbar and put one of the porch swings by the front door, with Skippy's rocker next to it—some comforts of home.

The mobile home was big. Skippy had the single bedroom, and Mama and Daddy were at the other end. In between there was a nice-size living room, kitchen, and two bathrooms. But it was very small for this family. Skippy soon realized that he could simulate an earthquake effect in the trailer by bouncing up and down in his room. This produced loud shouts of protest from Mama, who rarely left her bedroom in the other end of the trailer.

As workers appeared for the rebuilding process, Mama could not stand the constant parade of "perfect strangers" in their world. Strangers, perfect or imperfect, were never welcome in our life, nor were they dealt with easily. Now we had no choice, and Mama could not handle this. I took her to Virginia to stay with me until the house was rebuilt.

CHAPTER 10

THE ORDEAL

As the family situation in Florida worsened, I was flying there more and more frequently. Skippy's diabetes had caused him to be almost completely blind. I scheduled a trip home to accompany the family to an eye specialist for Skippy. We learned that he would have to have an eye transplant. This would have to be done at Shands Hospital in Gainesville, and Skippy would have to be hospitalized for several days. This was a relatively new procedure, and the odds for success were less than fifty per cent. Skippy could be permanently blind. We decided to take the risk.

The two-hour drive to Gainesville was a family ordeal. Even though she was not in good health, Mama insisted on going. Daddy drove the family car with Skippy in the front seat, protesting loudly that he was not going to the hospital, and Mama in the back seat with me, constantly telling Skippy to stop yelling. Brother William drove over from Tallahassee after work. We checked into the motel, but no one got any sleep that night–or the next several nights. When we got to the doctor's office the next day, we learned that the eye transplant had not arrived and probably would not be there for several days. This was unbelievable. We had no choice. We had to return home and make this same agonizing trip one week later.

When all was said and done, Skippy's surgery was successful and he could see again. But all was not well in Tallahassee, and I had much to think about on the way back to Virginia.

CHAPTER 11

GOING HOME

Over the previous ten years, I had built a very rewarding career as a staff director for the National Academy of Sciences, a prestigious scientific association in Washington, D.C. Mama and Daddy never quite understood my job in Washington, but it sounded impressive and they were very proud of me. They had instilled in me a hefty dose of self-confidence without being cocky and it served me well. I had enjoyed a successful career in Florida, but at the age of thirty-two, I decided Washington offered the best job opportunities, especially for women.

In 1968, with less than $100 in my bank account, and no job, I had left for the long drive to Washington. Daddy had two sisters I could stay with until I got settled. I clipped newspaper ads and started on my rounds. One ad was particularly interesting–the National Academy of Sciences was advertising for someone in their public affairs office. It required a degree in journalism, English, and at least one of the sciences. I had no degrees. I had gone to work immediately after high school. But that did not deter me from calling. I didn't get that job, but they later hired me in a different position, and I worked my way up to one of the highest levels, and most rewarding positions, at the Academy. It was a wonderful experience that I cherish.

There was never any doubt in my mind that I would eventually move back to Tallahassee. But I needed time, uninterrupted time, to focus on the issues, sort the priorities, and make plans. I had to be sure this was a smooth transition, with no regrets.

In early 1979, I took a leave of absence from the Academy and moved to my house in Orange, Virginia. Several years prior, I had invested in an old house in this small town about an hour's drive from Washington, D.C. It had become my retreat, a place to get back to basics, and I loved it. When my head cleared from the Gainesville ordeal, it became clear to me that I needed to be closer to home, perhaps not immediately, but in the near future. Meanwhile, I needed to say goodbye to Orange. So far, it had only been a weekend escape from the busy city. I needed to live there, for a while at least, before I could give it up.

I began a series of goodbyes, eventually leading to my return to Florida. My first tearful goodbye was to the Academy–to the building itself, which was a shrine to knowledge, to my challenging and rewarding experiences, and to the people, a very special breed. I found solace in the arms of the little clapboard house in Virginia. Actually, it wasn't so small. It was two stories, ten rooms.

Just to keep busy, I worked at a part-time job in a law office in Charlottesville, only twenty minutes from Orange. I spent the rest of the time puttering around

Orange and the Virginia countryside. I went to all-day auctions, county fairs and country craft shows. Mostly, I frequented "junk" stores and fed my passion for depression glass, but that's another story. I have such a vivid memory of one fall day when I found brilliant yellow and gold mums on sale for two dollars. I bought a dozen and put them in every room of the house. Then I sat in the front porch swing and admired my handiwork. I still have that porch swing.

Finally, it was time to say goodbye again, this time to Orange. But it was not time to move to Florida, yet. The house in Orange sold quickly, and the hands of fate led me to an adventure I will always cherish. It made the transition away from Orange much less painful.

One of my friends at work was looking for a roommate, and a house, so we teamed up and found a dream house on a place called Little Black Mountain. The next six months were the most adventurous, carefree, and spontaneous of my life. Linda and I lived with abandonment. We howled at the full moon, romped in the midnight snowfall, played charades until the wee hours, camped by the ocean, fished in the mountain streams, sipped high tea with our elderly landladies, and played croquet with someone who dressed like Alice in Wonderland. We were in wonderland. This was good for me. But after several emergency trips to Tallahassee, my crystal ball said it was time to get closer.

I planned an exploratory trip, which I combined with a visit to a dear friend in Jacksonville, Florida. Marilyn and I had worked together at the Academy in Washington before she married and moved to Jacksonville. During my visit with her, I realized how important it would be to have supportive friends when I moved back. And

Marilyn is one of the most supportive people I know. I decided that Jacksonville, which is about a three-hour drive from Tallahassee, would be a good interim move, so I said another tearful goodbye, to Linda and Little Black Mountain.

Jacksonville was a mixed experience. I tried to start my own business as a meeting planner. This was in the early 1980s, and no one had heard of meeting planners. They thought I was starting a singles group. I finally gave up and accepted a real job as meeting planner for an organization.

Meanwhile, Mama's dementia was getting worse. I heard about a geriatric specialist in Jacksonville who might be helpful. I forget how many visits we made, but there was no help. Mama was seeing several different doctors in Tallahassee, each of whom prescribed medications, and invariably she took the wrong dose. She became addicted to prescriptions. This was discovered in 1986 when she was scheduled for major surgery and she had to go through detox before having the surgery. She developed a blood clot in detox and almost died. I was making trips to Tallahassee once a week, sometimes twice. It was time—time for me to go home.

CHAPTER 12

800 HELP

Typical of their generation, my parents were very proud–too proud to ask for help, especially from strangers. Well, I am proud, too, but not too proud to ask for help. I asked, loud and clear, and someone heard. In March of 1994 I was the only caregiver panelist on Hillary Clinton's first healthcare forum in Tampa, Florida. Apparently I said the right things, because Mrs. Clinton invited me to repeat my comments as the opening speaker at the final forum, which was nationally televised, live from Washington. I later represented Florida in a video petition for presentation to Congress. Excerpts from my presentation were used to make a public service announcement that was aired on television and radio throughout the country.

Money, or lack of it, was a major problem. What little money my parents managed to save over the years had been quickly depleted, mostly for paying "sitters" by the hour, around the clock. Competent sitters were few and far between, and Daddy so disliked having strangers in the house all the time. His opinion of most sitters was best expressed when he said, "They *sit* real well!" The favorite pastime of many sitters was watching television or talking on the telephone, oblivious to anything else going on in the house. Lengthy phone conversations were particularly annoying to Daddy. He often threatened to have the phone removed. Sitters alone were costing us as much as $20,000 a year. We mortgaged my home, my parents' home, and Brother William's home. This money was used exclusively to pay for the care of Skippy and my parents. I exhausted all possible avenues of assistance. A local church trained volunteers to sit with Alzheimer's patients, and we welcomed the few hours of respite they provided. Friends and family helped whenever possible, but there's something about changing adult diapers that you just don't ask some folks to do.

One of the best sources of help came from a most unexpected source. Our funds were down to the last dollar, literally, and there was no help in sight. I found a publication that listed Alzheimer's research organizations with 800 phone numbers, and I began to call randomly. Most people politely explained that they had no funds to give to individuals, which is what I expected, but I kept going down the list. I was stunned when someone actually said they might be able to help. It was a lot of work, but this organization sponsored annual fund-raising events and allocated the money to assist selected Alzheimer's patients. I quickly completed the paperwork and received a check in time to pay the utility bill. Later that year, I was invited to speak at this group's national convention in Nashville, Tennessee, and was able to personally thank those who raised money for people like us.

CHAPTER 13

THE DEMISE

There is no cure for Alzheimer's, although drugs can sometimes slow its progress. Eventually, the deterioration of the mind begins to erode the body and its functions. Mama would forget when or how much she had eaten, so she would eat again, and again. This created all kinds of problems–upset stomach, malfunctioning colostomy, overload on the system.

She weighed almost two hundred pounds when she fell and broke her shoulder. Before recovering from that, she broke her hip. She never regained full use of either arm and never walked again without someone helping her.

Because of Alzheimer's, she did not remember that she could not walk. Someone had to be with her twenty-four hours a day. The hip replacement was medically successful, and she was released from the hospital in less than a week after surgery. A body brace covered her right leg from the knee to above the waist. She could not move, in bed or out of bed, without assistance, but she did not qualify for "skilled" care.

The only interim care facility with a vacancy was the local rehabilitation center. They had never before accepted a patient with Alzheimer's. I pleaded and they agreed to accept her on a trial basis, but we had to provide sitters around the clock to keep Mama in bed and calm.

After three days, Mama was responding to therapy and beginning to walk. We were encouraged, but it was short-lived. I was called into a meeting with the head doctor and officials of the rehabilitation center. They explained they could not keep Mama because Medicare would not pay to rehabilitate someone who could not "retain and carry over". I asked for an interpretation: She had to remember what they had taught her from one day to the next. It did not matter that she responded each day and did as they asked–she could not remember yesterday, and she had to leave. Mama was getting better, I explained, and she was responding to therapy. We had no other options. Their eyes avoided mine as they quoted Medicare rules again.

A tall, strong orderly pushed the wheelchair to our car. Mama tried to stand, but she could not walk. He lifted her into the front seat. We drove away. Mama never walked again.

CHAPTER 14

HOSTAGE

During the next several months, Mama's eating habits changed dramatically. She would say she had just eaten and refuse food. She wasted away to less than one hundred and twenty five pounds and still pushed food away with the explanation that she was "too fat". Finally, she lost her ability to swallow. First, she could not swallow pills. We crushed them into applesauce or pudding. Soon, she could not swallow food, and eventually, we gave her water with an eye-dropper.

In a family conference many months earlier, the decision had been made not to use life-support systems. As hard as it was to make that decision, it was so much harder to carry through with it. Hospice came in and tried to help us understand the dying process. We were new at this. No one in our immediate family had died yet. People used to just die. Now it is a process. Now they live longer and they die longer.

Daddy occasionally got some words mixed up a bit. This happened with hospice. In Daddy's language, the "hostage" people came to visit. As was the case with many of Daddy's words, his may have been more on target than the real word. We were, and Daddy was, hostage to Alzheimer's.

CHAPTER 15

CARING

Very early in our caregiving experience, Brother William and I realized the importance of "respite". One of us had to be on call at all times, and the other had to get away to recharge for the next shift. We dreaded the sound of the telephone ringing and never knew if we would find a life-threatening emergency or a disagreement with the sitter.

I remember one such midnight call from a sitter who said I had better get there right away. My house was right next door to the family home, so I was there within minutes. Daddy was in the living room, fully dressed, looking for the car keys because he had to drive to Panama City. He was adamant, and he was formidable. He had to meet a man in Panama City and nothing or no one was going to stop him. And he was taking Skippy with him. Skippy was awake and yelling that he didn't want to go to Panama City, which caused Daddy to shout even louder and demand the car keys.

After watching this scene for a few minutes, I realized that Daddy was hallucinating, caused by a new medicine he had just begun to take that day. This was more than I could handle, and I didn't know if Daddy would become violent. I called Brother William, who rushed over immediately. The sitter and I managed to get Skippy settled and assured him that neither he nor Daddy was going to Panama City. Brother William persuaded Daddy to sit with him in the swing on the porch and tried to distract him from talking about Panama City. The effect of the medicine slowly subsided, and Daddy agreed to go back to bed. Morning came very early that day, and it was difficult to face the "normal" world of getting ready for work. Nights like this put a strain on our full-time jobs, which were more than nine to five.

One of my pleas for help documented the enormous amount of time required to be a caregiver. I estimated an average of twenty to thirty hours a week devoted to dealing with insurance personnel or health care providers, arranging or accompanying someone to doctor appointments, managing checkbooks and finances. One of the agencies that provided some assistance required that their caseworker make "face contact" with Skippy at least once a month. I had to take three to four hours of annual leave from work to meet the caseworker at my parents' house so they could "see" Skippy and verify his existence. They always had a form that needed signing by a "responsible person". A sitter was not acceptable. Mama and Daddy did not understand why this stranger had to come into their house and ask questions. I had to be the responsible person.

Sometimes we needed more than a weekend to recharge and be ready to face the next crisis. After my turn at respite one weekend, my subconscious found a unique way to demonstrate this point. I was driving back home from a visit with my friend, Marilyn, in Jacksonville. Traffic on the interstate was heavy, and I soon noticed that everyone was passing me. Impatient drivers, I thought. But it got worse and I began to worry that something was wrong with the car. After a few minutes I discovered the problem: the closer I got to Tallahassee, the slower I was driving. The speedometer was actually showing twenty-five miles per hour! I was subconsciously resisting returning to the chaos!

CHAPTER 16

DIVERSIONS AND INDULGENCE

Subconsciously or not, I also knew it was important that I not lose "me" in the chaos. It would have been so easy to bury myself in the caregiver role. Nor did I want to be the martyr who gave up a career and sacrificed happiness for my family. I had always known that I would eventually return to Tallahassee. In my mind, it was predestined.

I didn't map it out, but I set about to build my life in Tallahassee. Tennis became a major part of my new life. I joined teams, made friends, and traveled to tournaments. I have never been a good tennis player, but, as one of my coaches said, I have determination!

My greatest indulgence was my house. Mama and Daddy gave me the vacant lot they owned next to their home. Logically, I should have built a practical, energy efficient, economical house. But that was too ordinary. I wanted something special, something that would fill my need for excitement, frivolity and spontaneity. I found all of that and more. I had exactly $40,000 and I needed to spend it wisely. I knew I could do this with my ingenuity and Daddy's help. In the process of looking at plans, I found a swim spa and built my house around that. The swim spa was a combination of a Jacuzzi and a lap pool that took up more than half of the wrap-around screened porch. In my rummaging around the countryside, I found three beautiful stained glass windows from an old church. One was badly broken, but Daddy used it to repair the two good ones. These were quite spectacular hanging above the French doors from the living area to the porch. I bought tongue-and-groove oak flooring from a local artist who also helped me with the blueprint for the house. I bought doors for one dollar each, vintage kitchen cabinets for fifty dollars, and a stove and dishwasher for twenty dollars each. As a surprise for me, Daddy refinished the old enamel bathtub they had relegated to the barn many years ago. The living area was one large room, surrounded by four French doors that opened out onto the porch and swim spa–nothing ordinary about this house.

I built the house with the thought of aging there, but that wasn't in the cards. After Mama, Daddy and Skippy died, I could not watch strangers go in and out of their home next door. Neither Brother William nor I would have been comfortable living in their home, and I didn't want to be a landlord. This feeling first bubbled up when sitters were constantly in and out of the family home–strange people, strange cars, strange noises. I could not have predicted this, but I also could not control the emotions it aroused. I put both houses up for sale and once again, I had to say goodbye to something I loved. But as has happened so much in the past, this served its purpose, and it will always have a place in my heart, and special memories of the many hours Daddy and I spent building it.

CHAPTER 17

A CRUEL BLOW

In his early eighties, Daddy amazed everyone by chopping wood, planting gardens, cutting the lawn, repairing the house–doing whatever he wanted to do. Then, shortly before Mama's death, he was brutally robbed, not only of money, but of his health, and almost his life.

An intruder broke into the house in the middle of the night. Everyone was asleep. While lying in his bed, Daddy was struck unconscious, and the culprit escaped in a matter of minutes. Daddy was rushed to the hospital where he was diagnosed with a severe concussion.

Typical of his tenacity, he struggled back to health, but never fully recovered. Later that year, he was diagnosed with prostate cancer, which was already at an advanced stage. Daddy dealt with this news by assuming that treatments would be effective and he would be well again. His doctor chose not to tell him differently. All of his life, Daddy had been able to fix almost anything, but he could not fix his health. This made him very angry.

After Mama's death, Daddy took care of Skippy with occasional sitters as needed, but as Daddy's condition got worse, he could not take care of himself or Skippy, and once again we needed around-the-clock sitters.

The cancer was steadily sapping Daddy's strength, but he continued to believe that he would get better. He kept his sense of humor and laughed and joked with the nurses and social workers who came by to visit. He had always said that he wanted to live to be one hundred, but he didn't make it. He died in 1996, a few months before his 90th birthday

CHAPTER 18

THE LAST TIME

Mama died over a long period of time, and Skippy had more time to adjust to losing her. Daddy's death in 1996 shocked Skippy. Daddy was Skippy's pal, his protector, and provider. Skippy was mad, mad at God, and told him so frequently.

Brother William and I were determined that Skippy would continue to live in the family home. We spent as much time as possible with him, but we had to keep our jobs. Our search for a live-in caregiver began. It was a journey of trial and error, mostly error. We soon realized it was impossible to find a live-in caregiver, and we settled for shift-workers. This meant a different person in the house with Skippy every eight hours. Brother William carefully prepared checklists, written instructions for meals and medication, schedules—written instructions for everything, but to no avail. Workers were late, or did not arrive, left early, brought their own children. One even brought bundles of dirty laundry to wash with our machine, and another took Skippy with him while he worked cleaning pools.

Medication would either drug Skippy so that he could not walk, or increase his agitation. It was a nightmare of indescribable proportion, and we thought it could not get worse. It did.

In November of 1998, Skippy developed pneumonia and had to be hospitalized. He vigorously objected, vocally and physically. Brother William and I took turns living in the hospital room with Skippy. One of us was there all the time, trying to calm him. Even with us there, he had to have restraints, but we were allowed to loosen the ties when he was not severely agitated. We were both at Skippy's side in the hospital when he died. We loosened the restraints for the last time.

END

EPILOG

OH NO! NOT ME!

I retired from my full-time job in 1995 and realized my longtime dream of being an independent meeting planner. I organized and directed statewide conventions, designed programs and registration material, and negotiated with hotels.

But best of all, I played tennis. I joined local leagues. Our team traveled to state and regional tournaments. One year, we were within one point of going to national.

That all changed about three years ago when I was diagnosed with early Parkinson's Disease. I was devastated. I had always dreaded Alzheimer's, but another disease had never crossed my mind. At first, I was in denial. I persuaded myself that I might have some of the symptoms, but nothing life-changing. Most people don't think Parkinson's is a serious disease. I used to be one of those people. Now I spend most of my time trying to understand the disease and how it will affect my life.

AUTHOR BIOGRAPHICAL

NOTE

A native of Tallahassee, Florida, Frances Hightower has extensive experience as primary caregiver for her family, and she has been a strong healthcare advocate at the state and national level. From the family caregiver's perspective, Frances cared for her mother, who died from complications of Alzheimer's at age 86; her father, who died from cancer at age 90; and an older brother who, despite physical and mental disabilities, lived in the family home until his death in 1998.

After an impressive career which included twelve years as a staff director for the National Academy of Sciences in Washington, D.C., Frances returned to Tallahassee and continued her healthcare activities.

She served as a member of the Florida Developmental Disabilities Council and as a consultant for the Claude Pepper Foundation and Florida Alliance for the Mentally Ill. She earned national recognition as an advocate and caregiver in 1994 when she spoke as the only caregiver on Hillary Clinton's nationally-televised healthcare forums. She has also spoken at several annual conferences of the Alzheimer's Association, and was presented a special award by the American Health Assistance Foundation.

Printed in the United States
By Bookmasters